Any Old Iron

15 cheery, light-hearted songs
Arranged by Gary Lerner

First Published 1989
© International Music Publications

Exclusive Distributors
International Music Publications
Southend Road, Woodford Green,
Essex IG8 8HN, England.

A1011105

215-2-576

ANY OLD IRON?

Words and Music by CHAS. COLLINS,
E. A. SHEPPARD and FRED TERRY

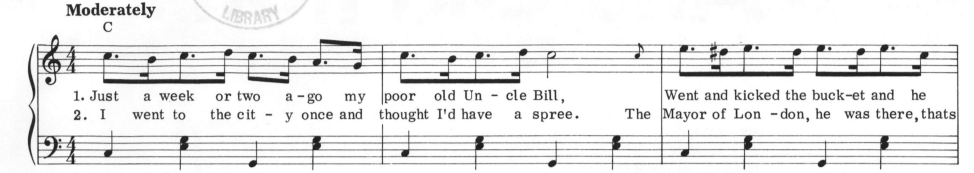

1. Just a week or two a-go my poor old Un-cle Bill, Went and kicked the buck-et and he
2. I went to the cit-y once and thought I'd have a spree. The Mayor of Lon-don, he was there, thats

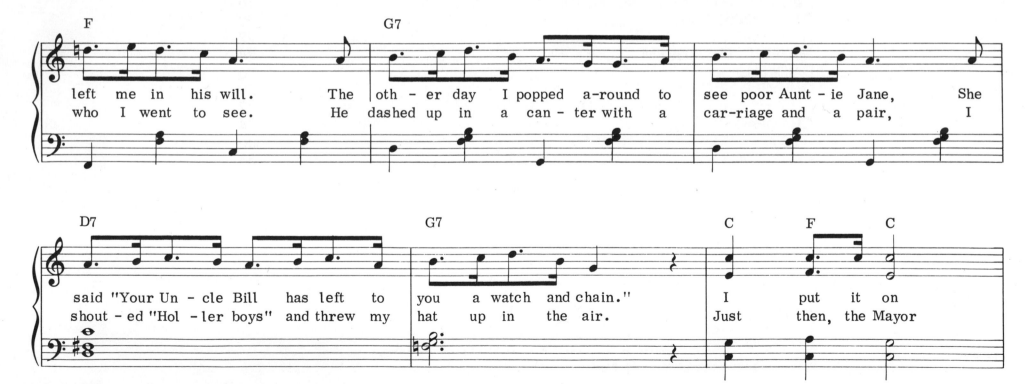

left me in his will. The oth-er day I popped a-round to see poor Aunt-ie Jane, She
who I went to see. He dashed up in a can-ter with a car-riage and a pair, I

said "Your Un-cle Bill has left to you a watch and chain." I put it on
shout-ed "Hol-ler boys" and threw my hat up in the air. Just then, the Mayor

OH! OH! ANTONIO

Words and Music by
C. W. MURPHY and DAN LIPTON

Waltz tempo, with a lilt

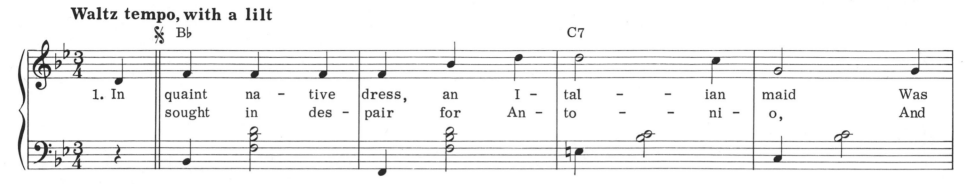

1. In quaint na-tive dress, an I-tal---ian maid, Was
sought in des-pair an for An-to---ni-o,

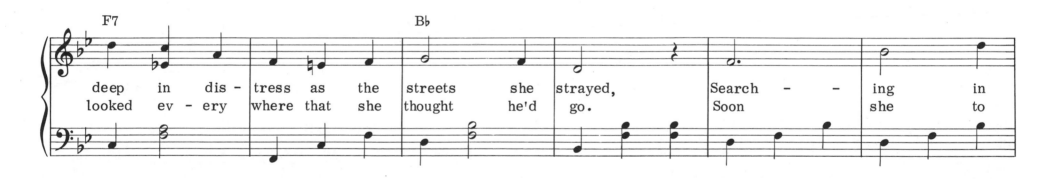

deep in dis-tress as the streets she strayed, Search---ing in
looked ev-ery where that she thought she'd go. Soon she to

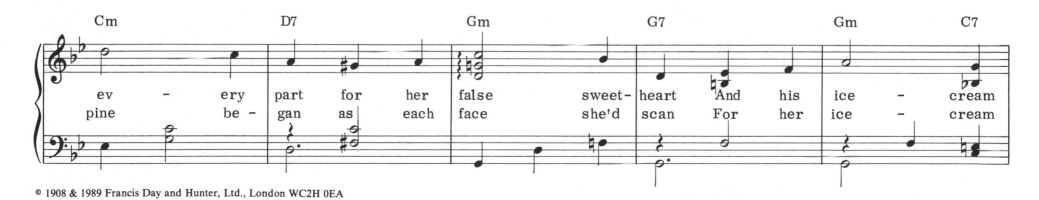

ev---ery part for her false sweet-heart And his ice---cream
pine be-gan as her each face she'd scan For her ice---cream

KNEES UP MOTHER BROWN!

Words and Music by
HARRIS WESTON and BERT LEE

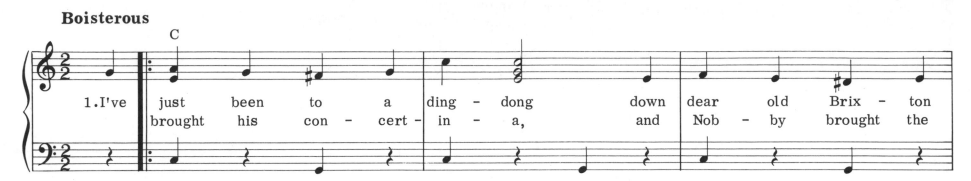

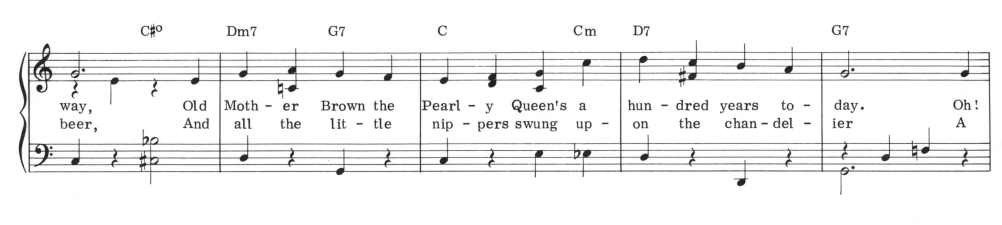

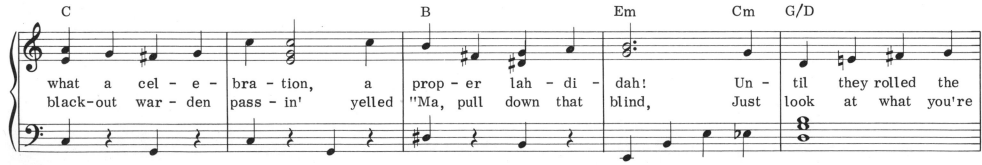

9

A NICE CUP OF TEA

Words by A. P. HERBERT
Music by HENRY SULLIVAN

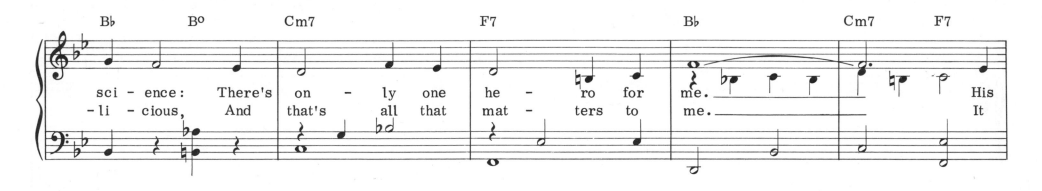

RUN, RABBIT, RUN

Words by NOEL GAY & RALPH BUTLER
Music by NOEL GAY

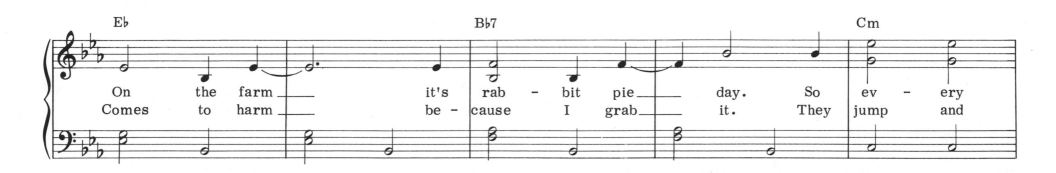

I DO LIKE TO BE BESIDE THE SEASIDE

Words and Music by
JOHN A GLOVER-KIND

Brightly

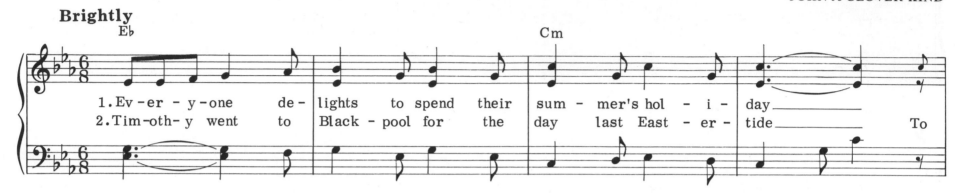

1. Ev-er-y-one de-lights to spend their sum-mer's hol-i-day
2. Tim-oth-y went to Black-pool for the day last East-er-tide _____ To

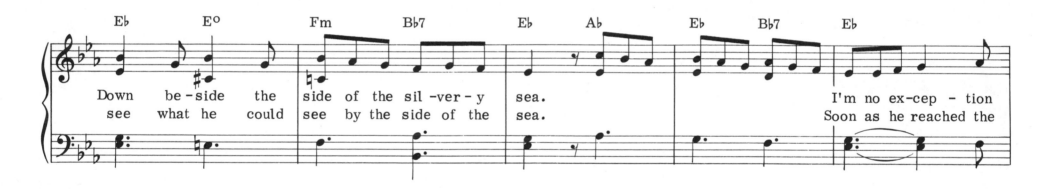

Down be-side the side of the sil-ver-y sea. I'm no ex-cep-tion
see what he could see by the side of the sea. Soon as he reached the

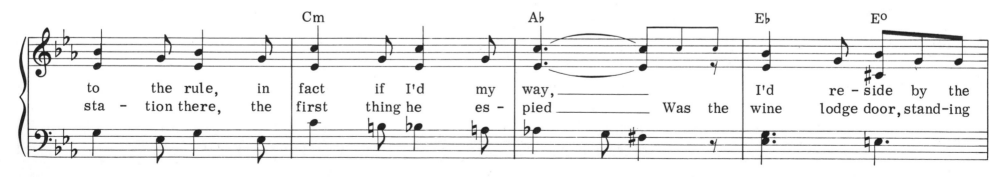

to the rule, in fact if I'd my way, _____ I'd re-side by the
sta-tion there, the first thing he es-pied _____ Was the wine lodge door, stand-ing

THE LAMBETH WALK

Words by DOUGLAS FURBER
Music by NOEL GAY

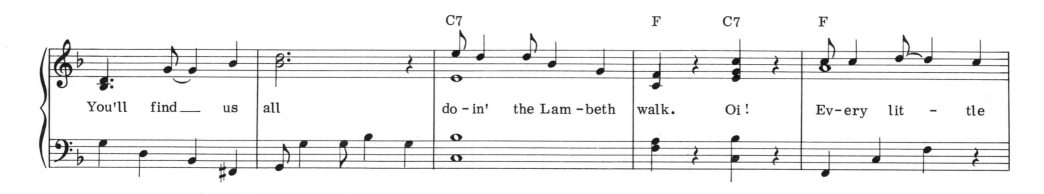

SIDE BY SIDE

Words and Music
by HARRY WOODS

MAYBE IT'S BECAUSE I'M A LONDONER

Words and Music
by HUBERT GREGG

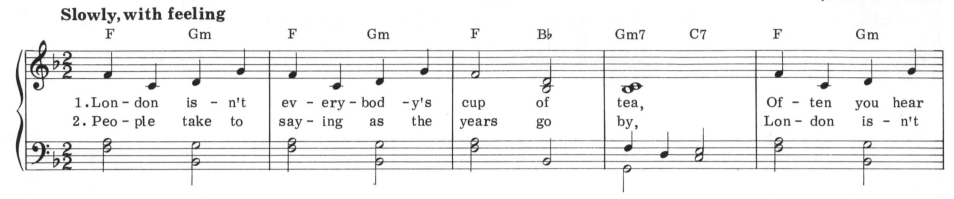

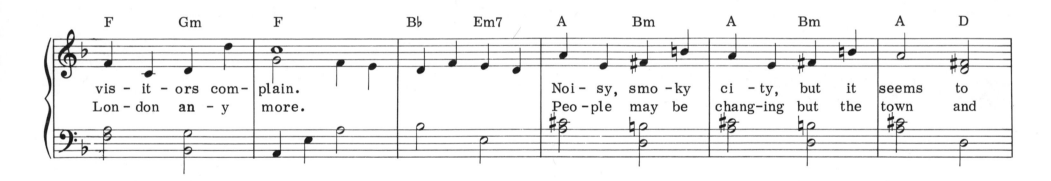

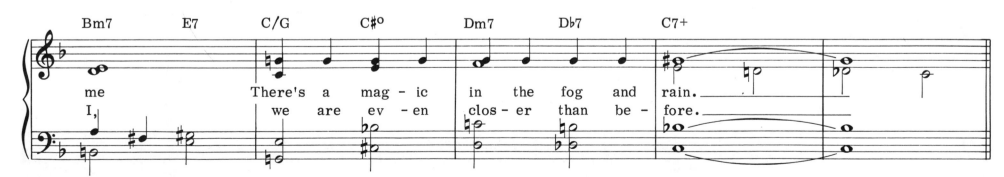

DAISY BELL

Words and Music
by HARRY DACRE

OH! MR PORTER

Words by THOMAS LE BRUNN
Music by GEORGE LE BRUNN

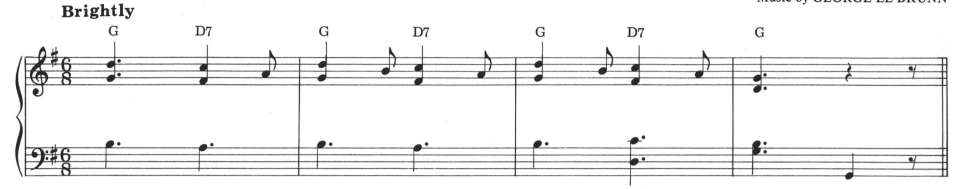

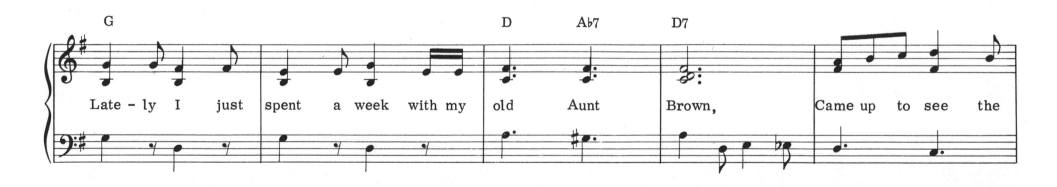

Late - ly I just spent a week with my old Aunt Brown, Came up to see the

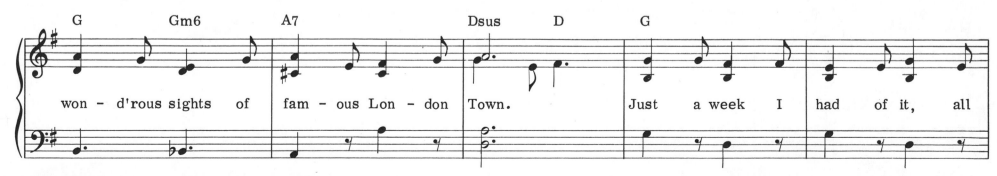

won - d'rous sights of fam - ous Lon - don Town. Just a week I had of it, all

HERE WE ARE! HERE WE ARE!! HERE WE ARE AGAIN!!!

Words and Music by
CHARLES KNIGHT and KENNETH LYLE

March tempo

Here we are! here we are!! here we are a-gain!!! There's

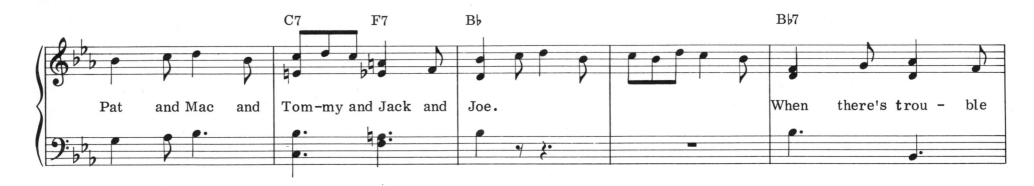

Pat and Mac and Tom-my and Jack and Joe. When there's trou - ble

brew-ing; ___ When there's some-thing do-ing, ___ Are we down - heart - ed?

CHAMPAGNE CHARLIE

Original words by GEORGE LEYBOURNE
Revised words by ERNEST IRVING & FRANK EYTON
Music by ALFRED LEE

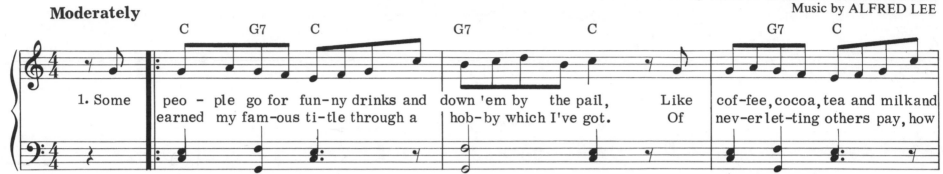

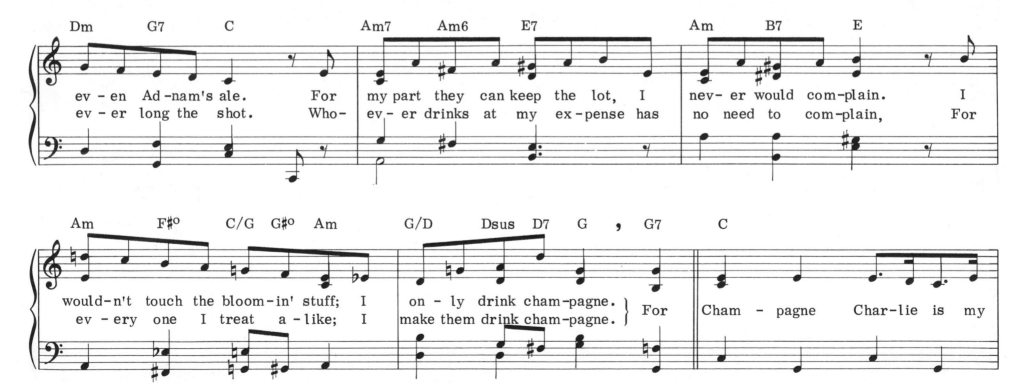

LET'S ALL GO DOWN THE STRAND

Words and Music by
C. W. MURPHY & H. CASTLING

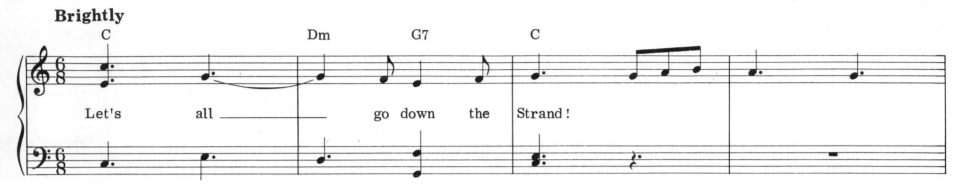

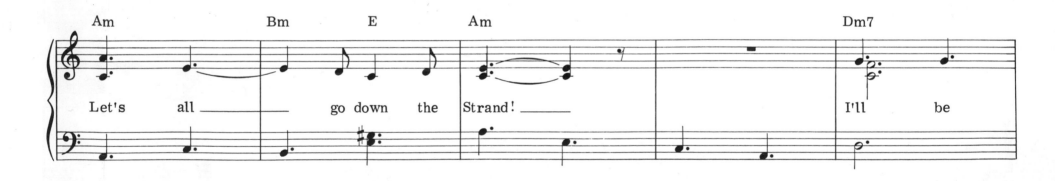

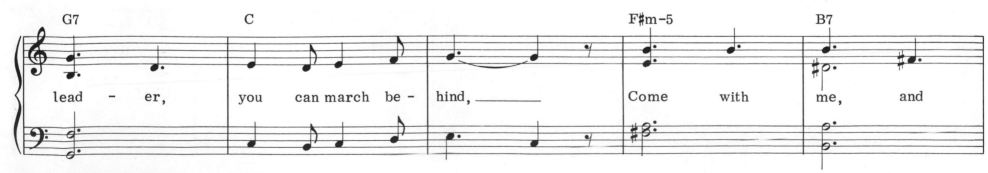

I'VE GOT A LOVELY BUNCH OF COCONUTS

Words and Music
by JACK SPADE

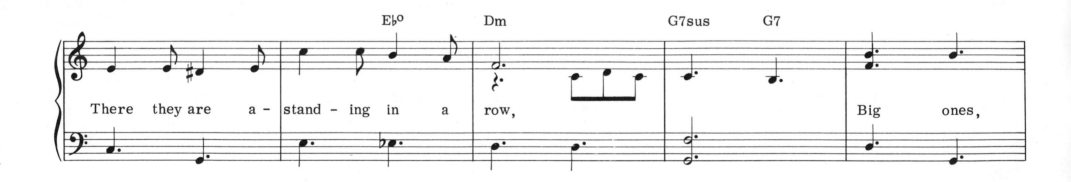

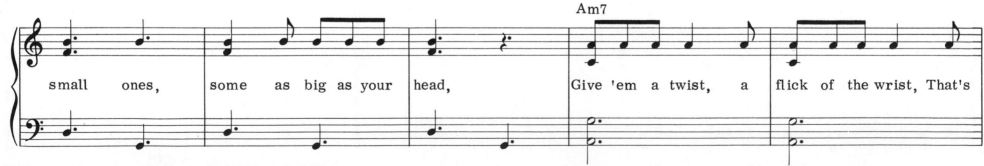

Printed by Halstan & Co. Ltd., Amersham, Bucks., England   11/95